To Roar Like the Lamb:

A Study in Sharing One's Faith

by

Arthur W. Fisher
WE Fish Ministry

DORRANCE
PUBLISHING CO
EST. 1920
PITTSBURGH, PENNSYLVANIA 15238

Dorrance Publishing Co
585 Alpha Drive
Pittsburgh, PA 15238
Visit our website at www.dorrancebookstore.com

ISBN: 979-8-88729-463-6
eISBN: 979-8-88729-963-1

Contents

Forward

Indeed, Pastor Fisher has given us a gift! In so reading and studying the relevant Scriptures, we who seek a deeper relationship with our heavenly Father are held to the Truth the Way and the Life that He intended us to grasp, follow, and live.

The format is helpful and elementary, yet essential and informational as a "road map" to the profound message and purpose of Jesus the Savior of the World. I have studied this book from cover to cover and would recommend its use as a catechism for all who desire to declare their faith in, and commitment to, Christ Jesus. It will also aid any who are seeking an instrument to use in teaching others to accept Jesus as their Lord and Savior.

I have also found it very helpful in my preparation for preaching and teaching. You will find it useful as you witness and testify to the saving knowledge found in Jesus. Sunday School and Bible Study teachers will keep it at hand as they prepare to proclaim the Gospel in a time when the Prince of Darkness continually tries to prevail against the Life of the World. I am grateful to Pastor Fisher for offering the church such a tool. Eager learners will understand the essentials of the faith and how to share them as directed by God. These 21 questions and 21 answers will aid you in effective evangelism by "Roaring like a Lamb."

Rt. Rev. G. Thomas Shelton
Bishop, Moravian Church in America
DeLeon Springs, Florida

Faith-Sharing

The intent of this study is to provide help for those who wish to be grounded in their faith, and then to gracefully share that faith with others. We'll do this by coming to understand Christian conversion and discipleship, and then we'll talk about how best, as individuals, we may lead another to Christ.

What is used in the teaching offered in this study are plain truths and essentials that are confirmed by Scripture. This study is but a "tool" to be used by those who are eager to learn the essentials of the faith and how to share it as we are directed by God. It is hopeful that this study will be just the beginning of a lifelong process of faithful discipleship and witnessing. The primary source for this learning is the Holy Bible. The fundamentals of this study come from the work of H. Eddie Fox and George E. Morris, both members of the World Methodist Evangelism Institute.

As you work your way through this study, I hope you come to understand Christian conversion and discipleship by answering the twenty-one questions that are designed to inspire conversation. It is best if you read the relevant Scripture in the order they are presented and read them in light of the question at the top of the page.

The apostle Paul expressed a prayer for faith-sharers
when he wrote to his dear friend, Philemon:
"I pray that your partnership in the faith might become
effective by an understanding of all that is good among us
in Christ." Philemon 6 (CEB)

What is a Christian?

Relevant Scripture: Acts 11:26

John 1:1–5; 14–18

John 14:8–11

Hebrews 1:1–3

Acts 11:26   Here we have the first biblical reference to "Christians." Disciples scattered out to many places after Stephen had been stoned to death. When the church in Jerusalem heard about how well the people in Antioch were coming to have faith in the Lord, Barnabas was dispatched to go check it out. When he arrived in Antioch, he was so thrilled at what he witnessed that he began teaching there as well. He then took off to find Saul—who was Paul—to bring him to Antioch to further strengthen the church there. It is said that large numbers of Jews and Gentiles came to the faith.

John 1:1–5   This passage echoes the Scriptural theme of creation. It also injects the idea of wisdom being the agent of that creation with Jesus being the Word and the Word being God. Jesus is revealed as the "self-expression" of God by being the Word. We should note that the Word is distinct from God (the Father) yet is also God (not god) and is the one through whom the world was created. Therefore, the Word is the giver of life and light to all.

John 1:14–18   Here we have God's presence revealed among his people. He made His home among them. For John the Baptist, he realized that his role was to bear witness to the fullness of grace and truth in Jesus. Verse 18 gives us the theme of the incarnation.

We have the Son, who is God, being the visible manifestation of the invisible God. The Word as the revelation of God.

John 14:8–11   Here, Jesus tells Philip the same thing he had told Thomas. He tells of the indwelling of the Father and the Son which tells us that the words and works of Jesus are in fact the words and works of the Father.

Hebrews 1:1–3   It's all brought together in this passage. In the past, God spoke to the people through prophets. The prophets weren't successful in maintaining the people's allegiance to God, so he sent himself—as His Son—to give the final word. The word was not given only in the sound of his voice but also in the action he took. God sent his Son to show us the way, the truth, and the life. **(see also Pr. 8: 22–31)**

So, bringing these passages together: **What is a Christian?**

Who is Jesus Christ?

Relevant Scripture: Acts 3:13–19

Acts 10:36–43

Acts 4:11–12

Colossians 1:15–20

John 1:1–5, 14–18

John 14:8–11

Acts 3:13–19   Peter is bringing to the attention of the people of Israel the role of Jesus as God's servant **(see Isa 52:13)**. Peter refers to Isaiah's description of a suffering servant because that is what the people know. Peter even mentions to the people their betrayal of Jesus **(see Lk 23:1–25)** as a contrast to what God has done for Jesus—his glorification through his resurrection. There is power in Jesus's name (v16). Peter understands the people's mistaken betrayal, sending Jesus to the cross, but this is how he assured them of God's plan for their salvation through His Son.

Acts 10:36–43   Understanding this passage emphasizes the need to keep all of what we read in the Bible in context to the whole. In this case, this speech by Peter comes after his vision that leads him to understand that all things are different now that Jesus has died and has been resurrected. He has been shown that all people matter **(see Acts 10:28)**. No longer should it be forbidden that a Jew associate with a Gentile. No longer should one be called impure or unclean. God is impartial—as Peter declares Jesus to be Lord of all. Through what is spoken of as the "Christ Event," God has fulfilled the Scriptural message of salvation through the power of the Holy Spirit with which God has anointed Jesus the Messiah.

Acts 4:11–12   Here we have mention of the building block that was rejected **(see Ps. 118:22)**. It is the stone God lifted up and put into place, calling it Jesus, the name where from within we find salvation.

Colossians 1:15–20   Inserted in Paul's letter to the church in Colossae is a song about the work of Christ. In this magnificent song of praise, we hear of Christ's supreme power over all of creation, including the new creation, which includes the church **(see vv18, 19)**. All things visible and invisible were created through him. It is Christ that holds all things together. All things are reconciled through the cross of Christ.

John 1:1–5   As in week one we learn that Jesus is God's Word… he is in fact God!

John 1:14–18   We have the Son, who is God, being the visible manifestation of the invisible God. The Word as the revelation of God.

John 14:8–11   The answer is found in vv8 and 9.

So, bringing these passages together: **Who is Jesus Christ?**

Who is the Holy Spirit?

Relevant Scripture: John 3:1–10

                        Romans 8:1–17

                        John 4:1–30

                        Acts 1:6–8; 2:1–13; 32–39

                        John 14:14–29

                        1 Corinthians 3:16; 12:13

                        John 15:26–27

                        1 Thessalonians 5:19

                        John 16:12–15

                        John 20:19–23

John 3:1–10   This very interesting conversation between Nicodemus and Jesus is all about the need to be born again. To have "rebirth" from above—the Spirit. There is symbolism throughout this passage and we can begin with the fact that Nicodemus came to Jesus when it was dark. Nicodemus was still in the dark about faith. He emphasizes to Jesus his understanding that he must be from God because of the miraculous signs he provides. He does not realize that Jesus is the light (enlightenment) he seeks. **(see 1:4–9; 8:12; 9:5)**

Entering the kingdom of God requires one to be transformed, which is comparable to being born again (anew). Jesus's message refers to receiving rebirth from above. The Greek translation for the term "anew" has a double meaning: "from above" and "again." Nicodemus hears only the "again" description, so he completely misses Jesus's meaning. Being born of the water and the Spirit is often associated with the provision of the Spirit through a water baptism. However, Jesus speaks of "anew" as being born of water and the Spirit (not receiving the Spirit through the water).

Wind and "Spirit" are translations of the same Greek word. This is why we often get the analogy of God's Spirit being like the wind… an unseen and powerful transforming force.

Romans 8:1–17 We are set free by the Spirit. This passage gives us a new principal governing our existence as believers. It is "the law of the Spirit of life" rather than the spirit of death **(see v6 and 7:13)**. The Spirit sanctifies us **(see v4 – explanation: 6:19, 6:22; 15:16)**. The Spirit leads us—if we allow him—which makes us sons and daughters of God **(see v14 and 16)**. This same Spirit will intercede for us when we are lost or stumble about **(see v26)**. The Spirit enables us to fulfill the righteous requirements of the law. By our human nature, the law convicts us of sin. God dealt with sin through His Son so that his Spirit could lead us to righteousness.

John 4:1–30 Another great story told as a dialogue—the method we are instructed to use when praying. This is a story of conversion. The woman at the well is from the marginalized part of society (we hear why during her conversation with Jesus). As was Nicodemus, this Samaritan woman was at odds with Jesus as a Jew. As Nicodemus came to Jesus under the cover of darkness, this woman came to the well at an odd time of the day. She came at noon—the hot part of the day. Early in the morning or early evening, when it was cooler, would have been the normal time to come. But this woman was an outcast and she wouldn't have been welcomed when most others would have come to the well. And this is why Jesus was there at that time.

Jesus speaks of "living water," which we know as meaning it provides "eternal life." This "living water" may also refer to the teaching of Jesus Christ, or even himself. It also may be referring to the Holy Spirit. V24 actually calls God, "Spirit," saying that "it is necessary to worship God in spirit and truth." Knowing that Jesus is the Truth and that he has come baptizing with the Spirit, the future is now and that true worship of God is possible anywhere for those who believe Jesus to be Messiah and have received the Spirit. V27–30 is where we learn that the woman has been converted as she leaves her water jar behind—that being her old way of life—so that she could go witness to the others in town, inviting them to come to the Lord.

Acts 1:6–8   We learn that our power will come from the Holy Spirit. The power is that of witnessing.

Acts 2:1–13   The coming of the Holy Spirit to "light" upon the disciples empowering them to witness to all peoples.

Acts 2:32–39   Peter's message at Pentecost talks of Jesus ascending to His Father's right side and his receiving of the Holy Spirit, which he proceeds to pour down upon those who believe.

John 14:14–29   The trinity is presented here.

Par·a·clete: (in Christian theology) the Holy Spirit as advocate or counselor **(John 14:16, 26)** The "companion" or paraclete for the Spirit of God means comforter, counselor (in particular: counsel for the defense). The Spirit of Truth will come to replace Jesus the Truth here on earth. The Spirit is with the disciples here but will not yet reside within them until Jesus breathes upon them (v20: 20). In v18 Jesus says "I will come." In v23 that has changed to "we will come."

1 Corinthians 3:16   A very definitive statement!

1 Corinthians 12:13   We are each an independent member of the whole. Without one another we cannot be whole.

John 15:26–27   The Spirit comes as an act of both the Father and the Son.

1 Thessalonians 5:19   This emphasizes the importance of the Spirit.

John 16:12–15   Jesus defining the Spirit and its role in our lives.

John 20:19–23   The commissioning of the disciples by giving them the promised Spirit and authorizing them to forgive sins.

Putting these passages together: **Who is the Holy Spirit?**

What are some of the names for the Holy Spirit that you have encountered?

What is the invitation to Christian discipleship?

Relevant Scripture: Mark 1:16–20; 3:13–15

Revelation 3:20

John 20:21–22

Matthew 11:28–30

Acts 1:8

Mark 1:16–20   Jesus starts off his gathering of disciples in a scandalous manner. First, he selects his disciples without input from those he selects. The accepted pattern was for a young Jewish man to select a Rabbi to follow and to learn from. When he made his selection, he would approach the Rabbi, ask to be his disciple, and then submit to questioning by that Rabbi as to his worthiness. Jesus, on the other hand, already knew the man's heart and selected those for delivering his Father's Word. He also caused some to leave their family business… something unheard of at the time.

Mark 3:13–15   Of his chosen followers (disciples), Jesus chose twelve to be "apostles." These were the ones he wanted to initially go out to proclaim the Word of God. However, it is important to note that their first and most important assignment was to be with him. **(see also: Mark 6:6b–13)**

Revelation 3:20   This is the end and the beginning. After Jesus talks of the seven churches and invites them to change their hearts and lives, he tells them that he waits for them. He is knocking on the door and waits… it is up to us to open up to him. If and when we do, he will enter our hearts and we will reside in his.

John 20:21–22   Jesus offers peace and then gives his disciples all of his authority (yet, he does not relinquish his authority). "As the Father sent me, so I am sending you." He then gives them his (and His Father's) Spirit.

Matthew 11:28–30   A key word in this passage is "yoke." Jesus's yoke is the Torah, which is the "light."

Acts 1:8   Jesus is teaching that their time will come when they receive the power of the Holy Spirit.

Putting these passages together: **What is the invitation to Christian discipleship?**

What is the mission of Jesus Christ?

Relevant Scripture: Mark 1:14–15

John 3:1–21

Mark 1:14–15   I don't think this needs much explanation. This is the same message that his cousin John was preaching.

John 3:1–21   This story of the coming to Jesus of Nicodemus gave Jesus the platform to describe for us what his purpose is. He starts with the necessity of "rebirth." Our hearts and minds must change if we are to enter into the kingdom of God. He points out that ignorance and misunderstanding must accept the truths that are brought before them through the Word of God. Faith must become the integral part of our life in order to remain anew.

If we view this in the context of the whole Bible, we know that Jesus is the kingdom of God. We know that we are born into a sinful world and that to be born anew brings us into God's kingdom here on earth, now knowing that we will have eternal life when our bodies are no longer available to us.

Putting these passages together: **What is the mission of Jesus Christ?**

What is the kingdom of God?

Relevant Scripture: Luke 11:1–4

Revelation 4:11

1 Corinthians 15:24–28

Matthew 25:31–46

Mark 1:14–15

Mark 13:24–33

Philippians 2:5–11

Luke 11:1–4   Prayer, first and foremost.

Revelation 4:11   All things were created by the will of God. The will of God is his kingdom.

1 Corinthians 15:24–28   God is the ultimate ruler and he is all authority. Jesus returns all things back to His Father.

Matthew 25:31–46   His kingdom includes those who are the widows and orphans, the weak, the poor, those in prison, those who are sick, and those who care for them. Those who neglect the least of His children will not be a part of his kingdom.

Mark 1:14–15   John's time of preaching was over. It was now time for Jesus to begin delivering the message. John had preached of a time to come; Jesus preached that the time had come. John preached of repentance for sins and baptism to wash it away; Jesus preached that the kingdom itself was at hand, so believe the gospel. John's message did not bear witness to the gospel; his message was that the gospel bearer was coming.

Mark 13:24–33   This talks of his return… both heaven and earth will be brought together and will pass away. However, His kingdom will remain. V31; "Heaven and earth will pass away, but my words will certainly not pass away." The Word(s) of God is his kingdom. Jesus is the kingdom!

Philippians 2:5–11   If we are to "Adopt the attitude that was in Christ Jesus," then we become the kingdom of God with him. Vv6–8 tells us how we should respond to that realization and vv9–11 explains the results. Our imitating Christ as our modus operandi will result in the "faith-sharing" we desire.

Bringing these passages together: **What is the Kingdom of God?**

What is Sin?

Relevant Scripture: Romans 3:9–18, 23

Romans 7:13–20

Psalm 51:1–5

Romans 3:9–18, 23   By these words we know that everything about us is sinful. I caution here to be wary of condemning ourselves and others. Even Jesus did not condemn the adulteress. Our natural tendencies cause us to sin.

Romans 7:13–20   Sin is a spiritual power of deception **(see v11, Ge. 3:1, 4)**.

Psalm 51:1–5   Sinfulness is naturally occurring. Our lives are filled with it.

Bringing these passages together: **What is sin?**

What Are the Effects of Sin?

Relevant Scripture: Mark 7:21–23

James 4:1–17

Romans 6:23

1 John 1:8–10

1 John 3:4

1 John 5:17

Mark 7:21–23 Sin manifests itself inside our hearts. Our actions and our words come from the heart **(see 4:10–13, 34)**.

James 4:1–17 I like James a lot… he is straightforward and for me his words are not minced. Words convey our attitude and our commitments. We cultivate our relationships with words… and we destroy them with words. When we judge, we place ourselves in God's place, which then places us within transgressions.

Romans 6:23 The choice is simple… sin brings death, righteousness brings eternal life.

1 John 1:8–10 Many say that they don't sin. This is untrue… we all sin. Sin comes from within, causing actions of unrighteousness that perpetuate more sin as we lie and deceive to cover our sins. It is never ending. Our escape from it is to turn to God, ask for forgiveness and live righteously to the best of our ability.

1 John 3:4 Rebellion portrays sin.

1 John 5:17 A difficult verse to reconcile. This, I believe, is talking about our judgment of someone's sin. Our duty is not to judge but to pray unceasingly.

Bringing these passages together: **What are the effects of sin?**

What is the good news (gospel/evangel)?

Relevant Scripture: John 3:16–17

Acts 10:36–43

2 Corinthians 5:17

John 3:16–17   When we read "…so loved" it is not meaning that God loved so much. It means that God loved in this way. This shows a giving God. One who cares for us in a manner that rescues us and gives us eternal life. God wants our salvation to be a result of his love for us, not a result of his judgment.

Acts 10:36–43   God is for everyone… he is impartial in all matters. The actions of Jesus are indicative of the power of the Holy Spirit that was bestowed upon him by His Heavenly Father. It is through Christ that God fulfills the Scriptural, and prophetic, message of salvation.

2 Corinthians 5:17   If we are in Christ and he in us, then we are part of the new creation where our old sinful ways have left us and righteousness has been invited into our hearts.

Bringing these passages together: **What is the good news that we should proclaim?**

What is grace?

Relevant Scripture: Matthew 11:28–30

Romans 5:6–8

Luke 15

Ephesians 2:4–9

John 3:16–17

Matthew 11:28–30 This is a very telling passage about who Jesus is. Here, he is telling us to come to him and let his life be our guide. See how he handles circumstances, with humility and compassion. The "yoke" Jesus is talking about is the Torah… the Mosaic Law. His life is his interpretation of that Law and his burden is life as the "light" unto the world. If we come to him to learn from him, we will find rest. We will find comfort and compassion for ourselves and for others.

Romans 5:6–8 All in God's time. There is a very basic and critical point to remember. Jesus is God incarnate. Whatever Jesus does, it is God. Whatever Jesus says, it is God. When the time was right (and at His chosen hour), God sacrificed His Son Jesus Christ who was himself. He did that for everyone. **(see Jn. 17:1)** All things occur within the plan of God. **(see Acts 2:23)** This concept is truly hard to comprehend. Understanding it helps us to answer the question, "Why?" One of the most critical values God has gifted us with is that of "Free Choice" or "Free Will." Our own free will. Everything works together… everything works as a lesson for whatever comes next. As we learn from Him and experience life, those things will come together and guide us forward. Even the timing of Jesus's birth and the circumstances surrounding that awesome event, was a lesson in God's love for us as He set into motion the changing of the world. **(see Gal. 4:4)**

Luke 15   All that is in this chapter leads us to the final two verses… In those two verses we, perhaps, are hearing the voice of God assuring us that he is always with us. And for those who are with him, he wants us to celebrate when someone comes to the family or returns to the family. Our celebration should make that someone feel extremely loved and we should feel his love as well. The changing of someone's heart is a reason for celebration.

Ephesians 2:4–9   This passage speaks of the great change from the bondage of sin to the freedom we experience when we live our life in Christ. The things we did wrong that are mentioned here are those transgressions (violations of God's will) we willfully commit. God's saving grace is shown to us in His Son Jesus Christ. God's mercy removes our misery and his love confers our salvation. We should understand that our salvation is not a "self-help" program. We do not and cannot earn it. We need only accept it as God's gift of grace that transforms us from being spiritually dead into a living and loving life.

John 3:16–17   We all know this passage, but do you know what is meant by "So loved"? It means that God "loved in this way." It is a descriptive of the character of God's love for us, that it's purposeful and giving. "Eternal life" is to mean "abundant life" in relation to Jesus, now and always! Jesus's purpose while here on earth was to save us, not to judge us. He had a lot of teaching to do while he walked on earth. His "judging" of us comes later, when he returns.

So, bringing these passages together: **What is grace?**

What is salvation?

Relevant Scripture: Mark 2:1–5

Mark 10:28–31, 45

Romans 5:15–21

2 Corinthians 5:18–21

Mark 2:1–5 The focus of this passage is that of faith in Jesus. "Faith" in verse 5 can be translated as "belief" or "trust." It is a faith that Jesus can and will act by the power of God. Jesus does not need to touch the paralytic being lowered through the roof. However, he does, which violates a taboo under which the people have lived. Jesus's ministry seemed to do a lot of that, didn't it?

Mark 10:28–31, 45 Being a follower of Jesus costs a great sacrifice. It may cost you your blood family, but the reward is a new family of faith. Looking at Mark 3:31–35, we learn that in Jesus's day, family loyalty was extremely important. We also learn that those who follow Jesus, those who do God's will, we have a new family that is actually more important than the biological family. **(see 3:31–35)** Jesus didn't come to be served, rather to serve and to give his life so that believers can be free.

Romans 5:15–21 Just as sin and death came through the action of one man, so, too, came the solution for sin and death through the action of one. As judgment came upon all of humanity through the failure of one, we find that all righteousness necessary for life has come upon us through the glory of one.

2 Corinthians 5:18–21 Being reconciled back to God is a result of achieving a "new life." We are entrusted with His message of love and reconciliation, which became necessary after the failure of one, so, we are to be ambassadors representing Christ.

So, bringing these passages together: **What is salvation?**

What is Christian conversion?

Relevant Scripture: Acts 26:18

Acts 9:1–22

Ephesians 4:22–24

Acts 26:18 A theological description of Paul's mission to spread the Word of God by drawing non-believers—Jews and Gentiles—to a place to receive the invitation from the Holy Spirit. Paul was building a community of believers which comes through God's transforming work.

Acts 9:1–22 This is Paul's story of conversion. It is not a description of what everyone should expect. Most people, I believe, will experience a more gradual conversion story. We could probably spend quite a bit of time discussing Paul's conversion and all that led up to it, the dramatic entrance of Christ in his life, and then the mission for which he was called.

Ephesians 4:22–24 Those who have accepted God's invitation, should understand that there are responsibilities. There are things we must do in order to experience the full expression of God's grace. Our hearts must be expressed in the life we lead. We must change from our old ways of living in deceit and corruption. We must renew our thinking and work toward becoming all that we can in Christ Jesus growing in the image of Jesus.

So, bringing those passages together: **What is Christian conversion?**

What is repentance?

Relevant Scripture: Psalm 51:1–14

Luke 3:1–14

Luke 15:17–20

Psalm 51:1–14 We must first seek repentance. In all humility, we should go to the Lord in prayer and ask for his forgiveness. Yes, we have been forgiven, however, the Lord our God wants to hear of our repentance. John Wesley calls our plea for forgiveness and transformation, a "renewing grace." God also wants to hear that our repentance includes our willingness to share his grace with others, bringing them back to him.

Luke 3:1–14   Repentance is about changing one's heart and life, moving away from sin and closer to God. John the Baptist was calling for repentance and preparation for the coming Messiah **(see Isa 40:3–4)** John also warned of having a false sense of confidence when he challenged those who came to him who did not seek a change in their lives. He called them "children of snakes." (v7) The fruit of our faith will be the expression of our repentance. That fruit will be inclusive of caring for others and doing what is right in the eyes of the Lord.

Luke 15:17–20   Because of his circumstances brought on by his life choices, God brought him to the point where repentance and a changed heart and life-choice brought him home.

So, bringing those passages together: **What is repentance?**

What is Christian faith?

Relevant Scripture: Acts 16:29–31

James 2:14–26

Ephesians 2:4–10

2 Corinthians 4:3–7

Acts 16:29–31 Believe in the Lord Jesus. Being aware of life circumstances and how they relate to God's movement in your life can bring you to that place of listening and responding.

James 2:14–26 James is adamant about one's faith being visible. If it is not, than to him, it is dead… it has no life, it has no value. If we merely profess that God exists and have a life that continues in wanted sin, then we in fact have no faith. We should put our faith into action…. We may be the only Bible a non-believer reads.

Ephesians 2:4–10 We are saved by God's grace which comes as a result of our visible faith. God freely gives as we should freely give. His grace comes first and we respond in likeness to Him.

2 Corinthians 4:3–7 We read here of being rooted in the Old Testament testimony that tells of an all-sufficient God. It talks of the old covenant bringing death so that the new covenant may bring life.

So, bringing these passages together: **What is Christian faith?**

What has Jesus done to make salvation possible?

Relevant Scripture: John 3:16–17

Colossians 2:11–15

Romans 8:31–39

Philippians 2:5

2 Corinthians 5:14–18; 8:9

John 3:16–17　　God's love is giving and purposeful. His objective while on earth was our salvation, not our judgment.

Colossians 2:11–15　　The circumcision spoken of here is the circumcision of our heart. This is what Christ did when he died on the cross for us. He removed our sins and set us free from the bondage of sin. We were no longer condemned.

Romans 8:31–39　　While our sins were indeed removed from our hearts, the consequences of our actions remain. Through Jesus Christ we have been given a means to deal with those consequences for nothing can defeat us if He is with us. Nothing can separate us from His love.

Philippians 2:5　　The mind (attitude) of Christ is the gift we received upon our justification and its manifestation in our love for our neighbor, which grows in power through the Holy Spirit in our sanctification.

2 Corinthians 5:14–18　　In Christ our whole human situation is transformed. By his resurrection, we have entered into the new creation.

2 Corinthians 8:9 He became poor so that we could become rich through his sacrifice.

So, bringing these passages together: **What has Jesus done to make salvation possible?**

What is the new birth?

Relevant Scripture: John 3:1–8; 14–17

Ephesians 2:1–5

In this passage we learn of the possibility of religious leaders being ignorant and misunderstanding the Word of God. And so are the laity. The religious leaders called him Rabbi, but that shows their incomplete faith as Jesus was much more than a teacher. Jesus explains the need to be transformed as in being re-born, in order to enter into the kingdom of God. Nicodemus's understanding of the Greek word for "anew" to mean "again" limited his understanding of what Jesus was talking about. The Greek word for "anew" also means "from above." Thus, Jesus's meaning of rebirth from above. "From above" initiates the Holy Spirit into the process of baptism which is the outward sign of the inward change – transformation.

John 3:14–17 Jesus is to be "lifted up" as a source of healing and life, just as Moses lifted the serpent.

Ephesians 2:1–5 A description of the change from the bondage of sin to the freedom found in Christ. Fallen humans indulging in sinful desires become spiritually dead. (These are the knowing participants being manipulated by Satan and his demons.) By nature these persons are subject to God's wrath but through his mercy, misery is removed and his love confers salvation. It must be noted here that salvation is not a "self-help" program. You cannot earn it. It is God's gift of grace that will transform you from your spiritual death to a living condition upon your acceptance of his gift.

So, bringing these passages together: **What is the new birth?**

How are we put right with God?

Relevant Scripture: Romans 5:1–2; 8:1

1 Corinthians 1:26–31

Review Scripture passages found on pages 26 and 28

Romans 5:1–2 We are made righteous through the expression of our faith in Him as it joins together with His eternal faith in us. Our faith joins His faith as we grow in our likeness of him.

Romans 8:1 If we are "in Christ" we will not be condemned.

1 Corinthians 1:26–31 Here we find God's revelation of strength and wisdom through weakness and folly. Coming to Christ foolish and ignorant, we have in him, wisdom. We grow in righteousness as we are transformed from His wrath, caused by our sin, into our new life received as we are justified. Our life then exhibits righteousness through our sanctification.

So, as we bring together these passage: **How are we put right with God?**

How do we become God's holy people?

Relevant Scripture: Romans 12:1–21

Ephesians 3:14–21; 4:12–16

1 Peter 2:9–10

Romans 12:1–21 As a response to God's mercy and grace we should give of ourselves completely in service to Him. We should not follow the ways of the world but rather allow our minds to be transformed by the Word of God. Utilize our gifts for the good of all and do it from the heart, do it with love.

Ephesians 3:14–21 Paul's prayer describes what our innerself should look like as we strive for "perfection" in Christ Jesus.

Ephesians 4:12–16 Christ's work was to equip God's people to work together to build up the body. It takes the gifts of all to come to unity on doctrine and experience and knowledge of Christ with the goal being conformity to the image of Christ.

1 Peter 2:9–10 Followers, believers, people of faith in Jesus Christ are God's chosen ones. We, together, become God's spiritual household. We become members of His holy priesthood proclaiming God's mighty deeds to the world.

So, bringing these passages together: **How do we become God's holy people?**

How can we know we are saved?

Relevant Scripture: John 10:27–30

2 Timothy 2:11–13

Romans 8:14–17, 31–39

Hebrews 10:23–25

Galatians 5:19–23

1 John 1:5–2:6

John 10:27–30 As lambs of God we are part of his flock, safe and secure with Jesus as our Shepherd.

2 Timothy 2:11–13 Forever faithful He will be. No matter the life we choose, God will always be there when we call.

Romans 8:14–17 By accepting God's Holy Spirit to reside within us, we become God's children and therefore heirs. Being heirs to the kingdom, we share all that there is with Jesus who also is God's child. He is our brother and as part of the "one body," we will be glorified with him as well.

Romans 8:31–39 Jesus has gone ahead to prepare a place for us next to our Father in heaven. In doing this, he expresses his love for us as His Father loves him. And as His Father loves him, so, too, His Father loves us. If our faith remains, we cannot be separated from the Father nor the Son. There is nothing created that can come between us.

Hebrews 10:23–25 Never give up on your faith because God will never give up on his faith in us. Stay connected to other believers as we are all part of the one body. Together we are stronger than we are apart. Hold each other in love and hold each other accountable to that love.

Galatians 5:19–23 Our selfish desires are what will keep us from inheriting the kingdom of God. Living by the Spirit will enable us to bear the fruit necessary for sustaining life.

1 John 1:5–2:6 We have here a declaration of God being the light, which represents his glory and truth. If we claim a close relationship with God yet live in darkness, then we live a lie. If His Spirit dwells within us, then we are immersed in His characteristics of glory and truth and our lives will be in right relationship with one another and with God. We are not sinless, claiming to be so is a lie and that will pull us away from God. Confessing our sin will bring upon us God's forgiveness and cleansing. This leads us to a life of humbleness, closeness, and active participation with God, guided there by Jesus as our mediator.

So, bringing these passages together: **How can we know we are saved?**

What are the marks of persons who are right with God?

Relevant Scripture: 1 Corinthians 12:31-13:13

Galatians 5:22–26

1 John 3:11–24

Corinthians 12:31 - 13:13   There is no better way to live life than to do so with love. Without love, you will have nothing. We each have gifts given to us by God, shown to us by the Holy Spirit. Our expression of love toward God will be shown in our using of these gifts and by using these gifts in love, we will show our love of God to others. [When all else has passed from our lives, what remains is faith, hope, and love. These are the sum of perfection here on earth. Love, being the greatest of these three things, is the sum of perfection in heaven. - John Wesley]

Galatians 5:22–26   Having a life filled by the Holy Spirit will be evidenced by the fruit of the Spirit that we produce. That being; love, joy, peace, patience, kindness, goodness, faithfulness, gentleness, and self-control. Being filled by the Holy Spirit and having no fear of it—other than "healthy fear"—our life will be led by the will of God.

1 John 3:11–24   Living a life of sacrificial love results in assurance before God even when your heart (conscience) is confusing you. God is the final judge of your heart... trust him and obey His commands. When you do that you will receive what you ask for.

Keeping His commands keeps us in God and then God will remain in us. We know this by experiencing His Spirit within us.

So, bringing these passages together: **What are the marks of persons who are right with God?**

What is the church of Jesus Christ?

Relevant Scripture: Matthew 16:13–20

Romans 1:6

John 17:18–23

1 Corinthians 1:9; 12:12–31

Matthew 16:13–20 We have the first declaration by Jesus of the establishment of his church. It is to be built upon Peter (Rock). Jesus anoints Peter with the authority of the keys to the kingdom of heaven.

Romans 1:6 Those who are called by Jesus are included among those who receive God's grace and are appointed as apostles. Members of the body.

John 17:18–23 This is part of Jesus's prayer in the Garden as he prepares for his arrest. He sends his disciples on a mission just as his was… incarnational. To go as a representative of the Father. The prayer focusses on the disciples remaining as one, dedicated to one another as he is dedicated to God and God to him, therefore, to them. The strength of the disciples can be found in the unity of the Father and the Son. Their goal is the conversion of the world to the knowledge of the Son as coming from the Father, demonstrating God's love for the world.

1 Corinthians 1:9 We were called by God to be partners with Jesus.

1 Corinthians 12:12–31 We are one body with many parts. All parts are necessary and are equal. We are all baptized with one Spirit—the same Spirit. We are the body of Christ, all of us together. We are all a part of one another, each with unique gifts that are to be shared with one another so that our one body will be complete. It should be our ambition, utilizing our gifts, to strive for the greatest of all the gifts—love.

So, bringing these passages together: **What is the church of Jesus Christ?**

www.ingramcontent.com/pod-product-compliance
Lightning Source LLC
Chambersburg PA
CBHW051337150726
47997CB00004B/1508